Abraham Lincoln

CROSSWORD PUZZLES

USA GRAB A PENCIL PRESS

CARLISLE, MASSACHUSETTS

Abraham Lincoln Crossword Puzzles

Copyright © 2014 Applewood Books, Inc.

ISBN : 978-0-9836416-1-2

Published by
GRAB A PENCIL PRESS
an imprint of Applewood Books
Carlisle, Massachusetts 01741
www.grabapencilpress.com

10 9 8 7 6 5 4 3 2 1

Manufactured in the United States of America

Abraham Lincoln
CROSSWORD PUZZLES

Born in a log cabin in Kentucky, Abraham Lincoln went on to be one of the country's most-honored presidents. Though receiving little education, Lincoln was an avid reader and oratorical master. Working his way up from boatman to soldier to lawyer to politician, Lincoln was elected as the 16th president of the United States in 1860. He had long championed the cause of emancipation, but was wary of the effect it would have on Southern minds. Though he sought a peaceful, equal, America, his election was met with secession, as several Southern states left the Union. And so began the Civil War.

Pitting North against South and brother against brother, years of battles and bloodshed left the country in shambles, with more than 600,000 casualties. President Lincoln worked to bring the nation back together with his memorable Gettysburg Address and Second Inaugural Address, which stated:

With malice toward none, with charity for all, with firmness in the right as God gives us to see the right, let us strive on to finish the work we are in, to bind up the nation's wounds, to care for him who shall have borne the battle and for his widow and his orphan, to do all which may achieve and cherish a just and lasting peace among ourselves and with all nations.

When the Civil War finally ended in Confederate surrender in 1865, many hoped the worst was behind them and looked forward to healing the nation's wounds. Days after the end of the war, President Lincoln was met with a standing ovation as he entered Ford's Theatre on April 14, 1865. Tragically, the same night, Lincoln was assassinated by actor John Wilkes Booth, and a frantic manhunt ensued.

But why did the Civil War happen? This book explores several causes of the war, from states' rights to slavery. It also provides profiles of the men who led hundreds of thousands into battle. Learn about Generals Ulysses S. Grant and Robert E. Lee, Stonewall Jackson and George McClellan, and learn about Jefferson Davis, the president of the Confederacy. Read the words that inspired a nation, honor the battlefields that saw so many fallen men and boys, and understand the war that split the nation in two. Open this book and follow the life and times of Abraham Lincoln.

PUZZLE ANSWERS ON BACK PAGES

Before the Presidency

ACROSS

2. Though his parents were illiterate, Abraham Lincoln learned to _____ and loved books

4. Some believe that Lincoln's first love was Ann _____, who died at the age of 22

5. With the advent of railroads, Lincoln served as a lawyer and lobbyist for the Illinois _____ Railroad

7. Lincoln worked as a shopkeeper, surveyor, and flatboatman, traveling down the _____ River

9. "Honest _____" was known for his honesty in the courtroom

10. Lincoln's father was the descendant of a weaver's apprentice who emigrated from this country

12. Born in this Southern state

14. The Lincoln family moved to this state in 1830

16. Lincoln's mother died when he was _____ years old. His father remarried, and Lincoln formed a strong attachment to his stepmother

DOWN

1. Won a murder trial by contradicting a witness who claimed to see the accused (Lincoln's client) by the light of the moon. Lincoln consulted this type of book, which showed that it would have been too dark to see

3. Lincoln lacked a formal _____, as his whole schooling added up to only one year

4. Some of Lincoln's favorite stories were "Aesop's Fables" and "_____ Crusoe"

6. Moved to _____, the capital of Illinois, to further his career as a lawyer

8. Served as a company commander in the Black _____ War

11. Became a _____ in 1836 after passing the bar examination

13. Lincoln spent much of his early life living in this type of house

15. Lincoln grew to be _____ feet four inches tall

Road to the White House

ACROSS

2. Andrew _____ was president when Abraham Lincoln entered politics

4. Elected to the Illinois State _____ in 1834

6. Lincoln published a book including his _____ with Stephen A. Douglas. The book was marketed during Lincoln's campaign

9. Lincoln ran for a _____ seat against Douglas in 1858. Lincoln lost, but he gained national recognition

11. Douglas pushed for a bill to allow slavery in all of the _____ Purchase

12. Lincoln joined this party, which had formed in response to the Kansas-Nebraska Act, which allowed settlers of these territories to decide whether to allow slavery

13. Lincoln was first a member of this party, now obsolete

15. During the 1860 presidential election, Lincoln won the _____ College vote — despite not winning one vote from the Deep South

16. Lincoln was nominated for president in 1860 during the Republican _____ Convention

17. Proposed a bill for the emancipation of slaves in the District of _____. The bill was never seriously considered

DOWN

1. During the Mexican War, Lincoln spoke against President James _____, who claimed the war started after Mexicans spilled American blood on American soil

3. Lincoln admired politicians Daniel Webster and Henry _____, who believed in a protective tariff and a national bank

5. After Lincoln's election as president, this state seceded from the Union before he was even inaugurated

7. Lobbied for Zachary _____ to become president, which he did

8. While a state legislator, Lincoln refused to vote for resolutions that defended _____ and condemned abolitionists

10. Served one term in the U.S. _____

14. Former Democrat Hannibal _____, a senator from Maine, was chosen as Lincoln's vice presidential running mate

The Lincoln Family

ACROSS

2. The Lincoln boys were known for causing mischief. Thomas and Willie once pretended to put a toy soldier on trial, asking their father to grant the doll a presidential _____, which he did

4. Robert studied at Phillips Exeter Academy and this Ivy League university

9. _____ was the eldest of the Lincoln children, and the only one to survive to adulthood

11. Mary's family objected to her _____ to Lincoln, believing him too poor to make her happy

12. Abraham and Mary's _____ was once broken off

by him. He suffered from depression until they reconciled and were married in 1842

13. After bouts of depression and erratic behavior, Mary was declared _____ in 1875, and her son Robert sent her to an asylum. She was released after only a few months, and the ruling was overturned

14. Some of Mary's relatives fought on the _____ side during the Civil War

16. The Lincolns had this number of children, all boys

17. Mary Todd's well-connected family came from this state

DOWN

1. Nickname of the Lincolns' son Thomas. Lincoln called him this because Thomas' large head reminded him of a tadpole

2. The Lincolns attended services at a _____ church but never officially joined a denomination

3. In 1870, _____ granted Mary an annual pension to help with expenses

5. Robert Todd Lincoln became a _____ in the Army and later served as secretary of war for Presidents Garfield and Arthur

6. Abraham and Mary Lincoln are buried side by side in this Illinois city

7. Mary also spoke this language

8. During the _____ War, son William died at the age of 11 of a typhoid-like disease. After his death, his mother often dreamed of him visiting her

10. After her husband's assassination, Mary lived in England and this other European country with their youngest son

15. The Armed _____ Retirement Home, also known as Soldiers' Home, was established in 1851 for disabled veterans. It became a retreat during the Civil War for President Lincoln and his family and is now known as President Lincoln's Cottage

Outbreak of War

ACROSS

2. During the Battle of _____, there were 36 casualties every two minutes for 12 hours. It was the bloodiest day of the war

5. Number of states that seceded after Lincoln's election

7. Antietam was the site of the first major Civil War battle to take place in the _____

9. Nurse Clara _____ narrowly escaped death when a bullet went through her sleeve. However, the bullet killed a soldier she was treating

10. Addressing Congress, Lincoln said, "Then, and thereby, the assailants of the Government, began the conflict of arms." He was referring to Confederate forces firing on Fort _____ in 1861

12. The Battle of Shiloh resulted in nearly 24,000 _____

14. Confederate forces led a _____ attack against Union soldiers at Shiloh, but they were defeated during the second day of battle

15. After the Union victory at Shiloh, forces moved on to this state

16. General Ulysses S. Grant led _____ forces during the Battle of Shiloh

18. The Second Battle of _____ took place in 1862

19. When it came to the Civil War and strategy, President Lincoln stated, "My policy is to have no _____"

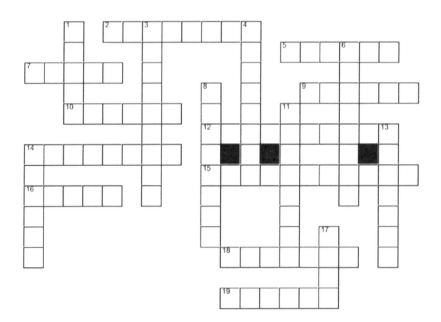

DOWN

1. In 1861, President Lincoln issued a blockade of Southern _____ and asked governors to gather troops

3. The Battle of Shiloh was fought in this Southern state in April 1862

4. In the South, the Battle of Bull Run was referred to as the Battle of _____

6. President Lincoln repeatedly changed commanders of the army in this rebellious state

8. The Union goal of the Seven Days' Battle was to capture _____, capital of the Confederacy. This ended in failure

11. During the war, President Lincoln and his family spent much time at what is now called President Lincoln's Cottage in Washington, D.C. The site was designated a _____ Monument in 2000

13. Oliver Wendell Holmes Jr., a future _____ Court justice, was wounded during the Battle of Antietam

14. Wade Hampton, J.E.B. _____, and P.G.T. Beauregard were Confederate leaders during the Battle of Bull Run

17. Union forces were defeated at the first Battle of Bull Run in _____ 1861

The Confederacy —Jefferson Davis, Robert E. Lee, and Stonewall Jackson

ACROSS

1. Jefferson Davis was born in this Southern state

5. Of secession, Davis famously stated: "All we ask is to be let _____"

6. Stonewall Jackson was accidentally shot by his own men. His left _____ was amputated, and he died days later from pneumonia

8. Robert E. Lee said, "It is well that war is so _____, lest we grow too fond of it"

9. Both Jefferson Davis' and Robert E. Lee's fathers fought in the American _____

12. When the Civil War started, Lee, who was originally against the _____ of states, was offered a command in the Union army. Lee reluctantly declined, deciding to lead the troops of his native state instead

13. Jackson and Lee were born in this Southern state

15. Jackson was very religious and did not like fighting on this day of the week

16. In 1859, abolitionist John Brown tried to start an uprising of

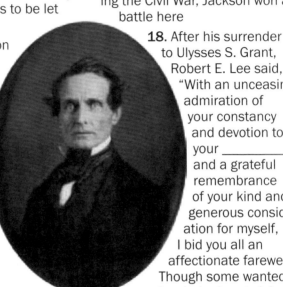

LIBRARY OF CONGRESS

Virginia slaves near _____ Ferry. Robert E. Lee was sent to stop him. This was considered a precursor to the Civil War. During the Civil War, Jackson won a battle here

18. After his surrender to Ulysses S. Grant, Robert E. Lee said, "With an unceasing admiration of your constancy and devotion to your _____, and a grateful remembrance of your kind and generous consideration for myself, I bid you all an affectionate farewell." Though some wanted Lee to be hanged, he was not punished

19. Before the Civil War, Lee fought in the Mexican War and then served in the U.S. Army's 2nd _____. Jackson served in the artillery in the Mexican War

20. Davis believed in states' rights and was opposed to increasing the power of the _____ government

DOWN

2. Davis advocated for the expansion of the Missouri _____, which permitted slavery in Missouri but not in other territories

3. Jackson was promoted to major _____ after several key victories. He earned his nickname "Stonewall" because of his relentless fighting during the Battle of Bull Run. Looking on, General Barnard Bee noted, "There is Jackson standing like a stone wall"

4. Robert E. Lee married Mary Ann Randolph Custis, a direct descendant of Martha Washington, the wife of the first _____ of the United States. The Lees had seven children

7. Lee was

given command of all Virginia's armies. He renamed his troops the Army of _____ Virginia

10. Lee became personal _____ adviser to Jefferson Davis in 1862

11. Like Lincoln and the Union, Davis and the Confederacy suspended the right of habeas _____

14. Davis served as chairman of the _____ committee on military affairs

17. Davis served as President Franklin Pierce's secretary of _____

LIBRARY OF CONGRESS _____

All the President's Men

ACROSS

2. Vice President Hannibal Hamlin was replaced with Andrew _____ during Lincoln's re-election campaign. Johnson was a Southern War Democrat who was against secession and supported emancipation

4. Simon Cameron served multiple terms as a senator from this state

5. Salmon P. Chase presided over the authorization of greenbacks, the country's first money made from this

7. Edward Bates, _____ general, remarked on the Cabinet's disconnect by saying, "In truth, it is not an administration but the separate and disjoined action of seven independent officers, each one ignorant of what his colleagues are doing"

9. Lincoln and Secretary of _____ William Seward became increasingly close during Lincoln's presidency, causing other Cabinet members to become jealous. Seward was stabbed by John Wilkes Booth's co-conspirator, Lewis Powell.

10. A New York politician remarked that "No _____ ever had a Cabinet of which the members were so independent, had so large individual followings, and were so inharmonious"

11. William Seward, one of Lincoln's former competitors for the White House, did not accept his nomination until President Lincoln's _____ Day

13. Montgomery Blair offered his _____ in 1862, but Lincoln did not accept it. Two years later, Lincoln asked Blair to leave for political reasons, which he did

16. Before becoming secretary of the _____, Salmon P. Chase served as senator and governor of Ohio. He also founded the Abolition Party and was a huge supporter of black rights

17. Andrew Johnson caused a scandal when he showed up

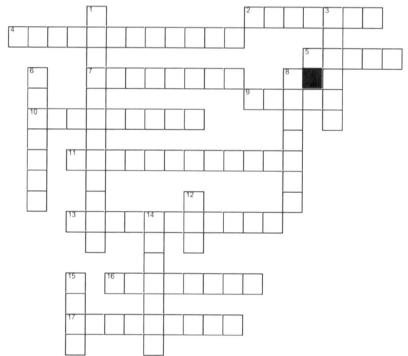

drunk to be sworn in as vice president. After becoming president following Lincoln's death, he was _____, but not convicted

DOWN

1. Of the slow movement of the government and his lack of influence, Vice President Hannibal Hamlin said, "I am only a fifth wheel of a coach and can do little for my friends." Though Hamlin was replaced in 1865, two of his children were at Ford's Theatre on the night Lincoln was _____

3. Montgomery Blair was against the emancipation of _____, making him disliked by colleagues in the Cabinet

6. Many of Lincoln's Cabinet members aspired to be president or sit on the _____ Court

8. Some of Lincoln's _____ members had been former political rivals, promised positions in order for Lincoln to secure the Republican nomination

12. Simon Cameron served as Lincoln's secretary of _____. It was remarked that he was "selfish and openly discourteous to the president. Obnoxious to the country." He was soon replaced

14. Postmaster _____ Montgomery Blair and Secretary of War Edwin Stanton were constantly at odds, with Stanton seldom granting Blair's requests

15. Edward Bates was a member of this political party, never converting to Republican like most of the others

Lincoln and Slavery

ACROSS

1. Speaking of slavery, Abraham Lincoln once said, "I believe the government cannot endure permanently half slave and half _____ "

5. In 1841, Lincoln took a steamboat trip on the _____ River. A group of slaves was also on board, and the image of them bound and shackled stayed with Lincoln for years

LIBRARY OF CONGRESS

6. Though opposed to slavery, Lincoln said there was "a physical difference between the white and black races which I believe will forever forbid the two races living together on terms of social and political _____ "

7. Lincoln believed slavery should be excluded from new _____

8. Frederick Douglass' original name was Frederick Augustus Washington Bailey. He changed his name after fleeing slavery and moving to this state, where he became part of the antislavery movement

10. Lincoln believed in protecting the _____ liberties of every resident, regardless of color

11. As a consultant to President Lincoln, Frederick Douglass proposed that former _____ fight for the Union army

12. President Lincoln issued the _____ Proclamation on January 1, 1863, though it applied only to states still under Confederate control

DOWN

1. One emancipation plan of Lincoln's called for the freeing of slaves and their colonization abroad. It also stated that slaveholders would be paid by the _____ government

2. The _____ Amendment, adopted in 1865, abolished slavery

3. During Reconstruction, some believed that _____ power should be transferred from former owners to slaves

4. After President Lincoln's election, the Crittenden Compromise was proposed in _____. It guaranteed the continuation of slavery in states where it already existed

8. There were nearly four _____ slaves at the time of President Lincoln's 1860 election

9. Speaking of the Civil War and slavery, President Lincoln stated, "My paramount object in this struggle is to save the Union, and is not either to save or to destroy slavery. If I could save the Union without freeing any slave I would do it; and if I could save it by freeing all the slaves I would do it; and if I could save it by freeing _____ and leaving others alone, I would also do that"

During the Civil War...

ACROSS

1. Georgia's Andersonville _____ became home to 33,000 men, making it the fifth-largest populated area in the South

6. The final battle of the war was won by the _____. It took time for news of General Robert E. Lee's surrender to reach all troops, and this battle occurred one month after Lee's surrender

8. Disease was rampant during the war. There were more than six _____ cases of disease among the Union troops

9. In 1864, the words "In God We Trust" first appeared on U.S. _____

10. In the Union army, black soldiers were paid _____ dollars per month while white soldiers were paid $13. In June 1864, both got a $3 raise

11. During his _____ Inaugural Address, President Lincoln said, "We are not enemies, but friends. We must not be enemies. Though passion may have strained it must not break our bonds of affection"

13. The first capital of the Confederacy was in this state

14. About _____ million people fought in the Civil War; 600,000 of them died

DOWN

2. Eighty percent of all wounds were inflicted by a _____-shot rifle

3. On the _____ side, more than 200,000 soldiers were 16 and younger

4. Men were not the only ones who fought. Hundreds of _____ disguised themselves as men and joined in battle

5. When Union General William Tecumseh Sherman was considered as a nominee for president during the 1884 Republican _____ Convention, he said, "I will not accept if nominated and will not serve if elected"

6. _____ forces captured Julia Grant, the wife of General Ulysses S. Grant, in late 1862. General Nathan Bedford Forrest, upon learning her identity, immediately released her

7. A naval battle between the North and South was fought off the coast of this European country. Citizens, including the artist Renoir, who created a painting of the battle, gathered to watch

8. The draft was first imposed during the Civil War, requiring men to join the _____

10. During the Civil War, approximately six _____ battles and skirmishes took place

12. Northerners named battles after bodies of _____, while Southerners named battles after nearby towns

The End of War

ACROSS

1. Only one _____ died during the Battle of Gettysburg — General George McClellan's sister-in-law, who was baking bread for Union troops

5. General George Armstrong _____ was among those who led 5,000 Union troops in one battle at Gettysburg. He was only 23 at the time

7. The "Louisiana Tigers" were rumored to be the toughest men fighting for the _____

11. This Southern state was so devastated by battle that General Robert E. Lee decided to move north. By the end of the war, more than 120 battles had been fought here

14. During Pickett's _____, an effort to attack the Union center at Gettysburg, two-thirds of the 12,000 Confederate soldiers were killed

15. The Battle of Gettysburg lasted _____ days and resulted in more than 50,000 casualties

DOWN

1. Some consider Lee's greatest victory to be at _____, Virginia. Here, Lee broke through Union forces led by General Joseph Hooker

2. The capture of Vicksburg resulted in control of this pivotal river, splitting the Confederacy in half

3. A _____ victory occurred at Cold Harbor, Virginia, a vital

Southern crossroads, in 1864 after a failed attack by General Ulysses S. Grant's forces

4. The last Siege of Vicksburg lasted from May 22 to July 4, 1863, when General John Pemberton surrendered. This was also _____ Day

6. In an effort to rid Georgia of General William Tecumseh Sherman's army, Confederate General John Bell Hood fought Union General George Thomas in this Tennessee city. The Union's counterattack resulted in a Confederate loss, and Hood later resigned

8. This side eventually won at Gettysburg

9. Union General _____

made several attempts to capture Vicksburg, all ending in failure until 1863, when Confederate forces surrendered

10. Sherman became famous for his "_____ to the sea," leaving Georgia in ruins

12. Wanting to end the war, President Lincoln traveled to Richmond, Virginia, the capital of the Confederacy, in _____ 1865. It was just days after the Confederate evacuation there and days before his assassination

13. The April 1865 battle at Appomattox Court House left Lee's army surrounded on _____ sides, forcing him to surrender

The Gettysburg Address

ACROSS

1. Four _____ and seven years ago

5. That this nation, _____ God, shall have a new birth of freedom

6. We are met on a great _____ of that war

8. It is for us the _____, rather, to be dedicated here to the unfinished work which they who fought here have thus far so nobly advanced

10. Testing whether that nation, or any nation so conceived and so dedicated, can long _____

11. Now we are engaged in a _____ civil war

12. Conceived in _____, and dedicated to the proposition

that all men are created equal

14. We have come to dedicate a portion of that field, as a final resting place for those who here gave their lives that that _____ might live

15. The _____ men, living and dead, who struggled here, have consecrated it, far above our poor power to add or detract

16. That from these honored dead we take increased devotion to that cause for which they gave the last full _____ of devotion

DOWN

2. Our fathers brought forth on this _____, a new nation

3. That we here highly resolve

that these _____ shall not have died in vain

4. It is altogether _____ and proper that we should do this

7. The world will little note, nor long _____ what we say here, but it can never forget what they did here

9. But, in a larger sense, we cannot dedicate — we cannot consecrate — we cannot hallow — this _____

10. And that government of the people, by the people, for the people, shall not perish from the _____

13. It is rather for us to be here dedicated to the great _____ remaining before us

The Assassination

ACROSS

4. A .44-_____ single-shot pistol was the weapon John Wilkes Booth used to assassinate Abraham Lincoln. Booth also had a Bowie knife in case the gunshot failed to kill the president

6. Instead of being taken to the _____ House, Lincoln was taken to William Petersen's house across the street from Ford's Theatre, where a dozen doctors worked to revive him

8. After shooting the president, Booth exclaimed, "Sic semper tyrannis," which means "Thus always to _____"

10. Booth broke a bone in his _____ leg after jumping from the presidential box to the stage

11. After the shooting, Secretary of _____ Edwin Stanton placed Washington, D.C., under martial law and ordered a massive manhunt for Booth and his accomplices

17. Booth, an actor, was best known for his work in plays by _____

18. Upon arriving at the theatre, Lincoln received a standing _____. This was just days after General Robert E. Lee had surrendered

19. During Lincoln's final speech, on April 11, Booth confided to a friend: "That is the _____ speech he will ever give"

DOWN

1. John Wilkes Booth's _____, Junius Brutus Booth, was a famous English tragedian actor

2. Booth was found, shot, and killed on April 26, 1865, in a barn in this Southern state

3. Union General Ulysses S. _____ and his wife were invited to attend the play at Ford's Theatre, but they left Washington, D.C., earlier in the day

5. Just days before giving his _____ Address, Lincoln attended a performance by Booth at Ford's Theatre

7. Lincoln, who was given mouth-to-mouth resuscitation by a 23-year-old army doctor, temporarily started _____ again on his own

9. Lincoln started going to Ford's Theatre in 1862, saying, "Some think I do wrong to go to the opera and theater, but it relieves my heavy _____"

12. A $100,000 _____ was offered for the capture of Booth, who eluded the government for nearly two weeks

13. Mary Todd Lincoln's confidante, after listening to Lincoln's last speech given in the open air, remarked: "What an easy matter would it be to kill the _____"

14. The play that was performed on the night of Lincoln's assassination was "Our _____ Cousin"

15. Lincoln was shot on the religious holiday of Good _____ and died the next morning, April 15, 1865

16. Conspirators met at the boardinghouse of Mary Surratt, who became the first _____ to be executed by the U.S. government

The Words of Lincoln

ACROSS

5. When you reach the end of your _____, tie a knot and hang on

6. When I do good, I feel good. When I do bad, I feel bad. That's my _____

7. With malice toward none, with charity for all, with firmness in the right as God gives us to see the right, let us strive on to finish the work we are in, to bind up the nation's wounds, to care for him who shall have borne the battle and for his widow and his orphan, to do all which may achieve and cherish a just and lasting _____ among ourselves and with all nations

8. Whenever I hear anyone arguing for _____, I feel a strong impulse to see it tried on him personally

10. I have been driven many times to my knees by the overwhelming conviction that I had _____ else to go

11. Whatever you are, be a _____ one

12. America will never be destroyed from the outside. If we falter and lose our freedoms, it will be because we destroyed _____

15. The ballot is _____ than the bullet

16. And in the end it is not the years in your life that count, it's the life in your _____

17. Gentlemen, why do you not laugh? With the fearful strain that is upon me day and _____, if I did not laugh, I should die

DOWN

1. Both read the same _____ and pray to the same God, and each invokes His aid against the other. It may seem strange that any men should dare to ask a just God's assistance in wringing their bread from the sweat of other men's faces, but let us judge not, that we be not judged. The prayers of both could not be answered. That of neither has been answered fully. The Almighty has His own purposes

2. You cannot help men permanently by doing for them, what they could and should do for

_____

3. The best way to destroy an enemy is to make him a _____

4. It is better to remain _____ and be thought a fool than to open one's mouth and remove all doubt

9. You can please some of the people some of the time, all of the people some of the time, some of the people all of the time, but you can never please all of the people _____ of the time

13. We can complain because rose bushes have thorns, or rejoice because thorn bushes have

_____

14. A house divided against itself cannot _____

18. People are just as _____ as they make up their minds to be

PUZZLE ANSWERS

Before the Presidency

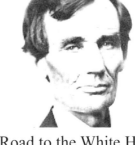

Road to the White House

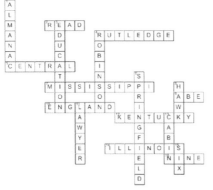

The Lincoln Family

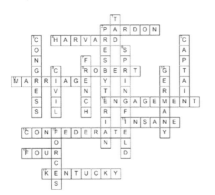

Outbreak of War

The Confederacy

All the President's Men

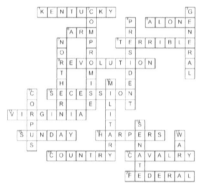

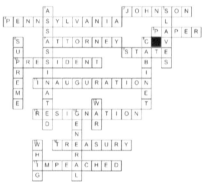

Lincoln and Slavery

During the Civil War ...

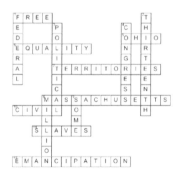

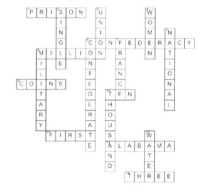

The End of War

The Gettysburg Address

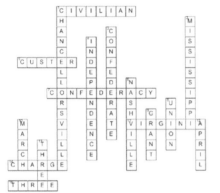

The Assassination

The Words of Lincoln

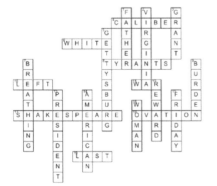

TITLES FROM
GRAB A PENCIL PRESS

Abraham Lincoln Crossword Puzzles

American Revolution Crossword Puzzles

Architecture Crossword Puzzles

Art History Puzzle Book

Benjamin Franklin Puzzle Book

Civil War History Crossword Puzzles

Ellis Island and the Statue of Liberty Crossword Puzzles

George Washington Crossword Puzzles

John Fitzgerald Kennedy Crossword Puzzles

Natural History Activity Book

New York City Crossword Puzzles

Presidents of the United States Crossword Puzzles

Texas History Crossword Puzzles

Washington, D.C. Puzzle Book

Yellowstone National Park Puzzle Book

USA GRAB A PENCIL PRESS

an imprint of Applewood Books
Carlisle, Massachusetts 01741
www.grabapencilpress.com
800.277.5312